Hubert Huber

THE
CREATION

REVOLT OF THE CREATED

All for the greater glory of God

For the youth of the world

The author

Hubertus Huber was born in 1938 in Freiburg i. Br. His religion teacher was Dr. Ernst Föhr, later vicar general of Archbishop Schäufele in Freiburg. Dr. Föhr explained to his student: the Church is always attacked by Satan.

"As long as we can eliminate the heretics (unbelievers) in time, the Holy Church will not change. If it does not succeed, it will develop into a sect."

This was said by Dr. Föhr in 1955, 10 years before the Council. It did not succeed in eliminating the heretics. A great guilt for the decay of the Church is borne by those who, by their silence, covered for the heretics and thus supported them.

In 1969, leaving Sunday Mass, for the first time at the "people's altar" and with instructions for hand communion, an elderly gentleman said, "This is a new republic."

What do you mean, the author wanted to know? The gentleman replied, "Christ the King has been overthrown. His enemies are taking over the leadership in the Church. They will open the door to evil".

Since then, the author has observed the disintegration of the Church and has tried to document this development.

Table of Contents   Page

The Creation

In the beginning was the Word (the Son of God) and the Word was with God, and God was the Word. Even in the beginning, It was with God. Through the Word all things came to be, and nothing that came to be was without the Word. In Him was the life, and the life was the light of men. And the light shone in the darkness (of sin); but the darkness did not understand it. There was a man sent from God; his name was John. This man came as a witness; he was to bear witness to the light, so that all might come to faith through him. He himself was not the light, he was only to give testimony of the light. This was the true light that enlightens every person who comes into this world. He (Christ) was in the world, and the world became through him. But the world did not recognize him. He came into its possession, but His own did not receive Him. But to all who received Him, He gave power to become children of God, to all who believe in His name, who were born, not of blood, nor of the desire of the flesh, nor of the will of man, but of God. And the Word became flesh and dwelt among us. And we have seen His glory, the glory of the only begotten of the Father, full of grace and truth. Thanks be to God. (John 1:1-14)

This Gospel of John, was read after every Holy Mass, according to the bull "Quo primum" of 17.7.1570, of St. Pope Pius V. After the Council, this Gospel was deleted.

As children of God, we must receive Jesus and live in His grace. However, Jesus remains with us only if we accept

His teachings and commandments unchanged. **The Lamb of God cannot come where Satan has left his mark.**

The Creation of the World - The Test of the Angels, Venerable Sister Mary of Agreda

God is the cause of all beings, their Creator. He willed to begin the extra-Trinitarian marvels of His omnipotence, as and when it pleases His free divine will. Moses tells about it in the first chapter of Genesis. Since the Lord enlightened me about it, I will say what is necessary here, so that the works and mysteries of the incarnation of the divine Word and the redemption from the origin may be recognized.

In the first chapter of Genesis it says: "In the beginning God created the heavens and the earth. But the earth was desolate and empty. Darkness was over the abyss, and the Spirit of God hovered over the waters. Then God said, "Let there be light!" And there was light. And God saw that the light was good, and He separated the light from the darkness. And He called the light Day and the darkness Night. And there was evening and morning, the first day" (Gen. 1:1-5) On that first day - Moses says "in the beginning" - God created the heavens and the earth. In this beginning, the almighty God, persisting in His immutability, stepped out of Himself, as it were, to give creatures an existence of their own. He began, as it were, to take pleasure in His creatures as in works that were perfect in their way. In order that the order of creation be a most perfect one, He created heaven for the angels and men before the rational beings, and the earth as a dwelling place for men during their pilgrimage. Both places He created so perfectly and according to their God-ordained purposes that David could sing: "The heavens tell the glory of God, of the work of His hands the vault of the heavens tells!" (Ps.t 18:2). The heavens in their beauty reveal the greatness and glory of God. They are the reward that the Lord has prepared in advance for His saints. The universe of the earth indicates that people should dwell there and walk on it to their Creator. Before their creation, He prepared everything for them and drew out of nothing what was necessary for their life and purpose. Through all this they should feel obliged to obey their Creator and Benefactor, to love Him and to recognize His wonderful name together with His infinite perfection from His works.

Moses says of the earth that it was desolate and empty. He does not say that of heaven. There God created the angels. Moses indicated it with the word: "God said: Let there be light! And the light was." Moses is not only talking about the material light, but also about the angels, these spiritual lights. He does not express himself clearly here, because the Jews were often inclined to ascribe divine beingness to extraordinary things, even if they were far below the angels in dignity. However, the symbol >light< was very significant for the nature of the angels, also with regard to their knowledge and their graces, by which they were already radiated at their creation. **At the same time God created the earth and in its center the hell**. According to God's will, very deep and wide crypts were created for hell, limbo and purgatory. In hell, a material fire was created, as well as everything that is now used to torment the damned. Then the Lord separated the light from the darkness and called the latter day, but the latter night. The separation took place not only between day and night in nature, but also between the good and the evil angels. To the good ones He gave the eternal light of His sight and called it day, eternal day. The evil ones, on the other hand, He called night of sin and hurled them into the eternal darkness of hell. From this we can see how the merciful generosity of the Creator and Living Maker and the justice of the righteous Judge unite.

The angels were created in the empyrean (light) heaven, in the state of grace. With this, they were to earn glory as a reward. Although they were in the place of grace, they did not see the Godhead face to face until they had earned it with grace through obedience to the divine will. The good as well as the apostate angels remained only a short time in the state of trial, because the creation, trial and decision took place in three very short periods of time. In the first period, all the angels were created and endowed with grace and the gifts of the Holy Spirit, so that they were exceedingly beautiful and perfect. Then followed a short period in which the will of the Creator was made known to all. They received the law and the order to acknowledge their Creator as their supreme Lord and thus fulfill the purpose of their existence. In this short while, St. Michael and his angels had that great conflict against the dragon and his followers, which St. John reports in the 12th chapter of the Secret Revelation. **The good angels earned eternal bliss through perseverance in grace, while the disobedient ones fell into eternal torment through their rebellion against God.**

According to the nature of the angelic nature and by virtue of God's omnipotence, all this could have happened very quickly in the second period. But I realized that the compassionate goodness of the Most High, with a certain hesitant lingering, presented to the angels the good and evil, true and false, just and unjust, as well as the wickedness of sin and the enmity of God, the eternal reward and the eternal punishment, finally also the rejection of Lucifer and his followers. His divine majesty showed them hell and its chastisement. They saw everything; for in their sublime, purely spiritual nature they can clearly recognize all created, finite things as these are in themselves, i.e. according to their essence. In this ability they saw and recognized clearly the place of punishment before the fall from grace. But they could not recognize the reward of glory in this way. But they received a different knowledge of it and, moreover, a revealed, explicit promise from the Lord Himself. Thereby the Most High had justified His cause and acted most righteously. All this goodness and justice, however, did not hold back Lucifer and his followers. That is why they were chastised as hardened ones and hurled into the depth of hell. On the other hand, the good angels were eternally fortified in grace and glory. All this happened in the third period. Thus it is proved that, apart from God, no being is by nature incapable of sinning; for the angels sinned in spite of their exalted nature, endowed with such high knowledge and so many graces. They were lost. What will be the fate of human frailty if God's omnipotence does not protect it, and if man forces God, as it were, to abandon Him?

I wished to know for what motive and by what cause Lucifer and his followers were disobedient and fell. I realized that the evil angels could commit many crimes according to the guilt (secundum reatum), even if they did not commit all of them according to the deed. That sin, however, which they actually committed with their evil will, produced in them the habitus, i.e. the inclination to all evil. Also to that, which they could not commit themselves. To these sins, however, they seduce the people and rejoice when they succeed. Lucifer got into a very disordered self-love at that time; because he saw himself equipped with a higher beauty of nature and grace than the other angels. In this realization he lingered too long, and the pleasure in himself so restrained him, that he offered to God, the sole cause of all his excellences, the thanks he owed, casually and indolently. Again he looked at himself. His beauty and his graces pleased him anew. He attributed them to himself and loved them as his own. This disordered self-contemplation caused him not only to raise himself above himself with the powers he had received from a higher power - not as he should have done - but it also led him to envy against others and to lust after the gifts and merits of others. Since he could not obtain these for himself, he was inflamed with deadly anger and hatred against God, who had created him from nothing, and against all His creatures.

From this condition sprang disobedience, presumption, injustice, disloyalty, blasphemy, even a kind of idolatry; for he desired for himself that worship which is owed to God alone. He blasphemed God's majesty and holiness. He lost faith and guilty fidelity. He presumptuously planned to destroy all creatures and flattered himself that he could do this and many other things. He remained in this state of mind. His arrogance increased. But his presumption was greater than his strength; for in this he could not grow, but with regard to sin "one abyss calls to another" (Ps.41:8).

The first sinful angel was Lucifer, as Isaias tells us in the 14th chapter. He seduced the others. That is why he is called the prince of evil spirits, not because of his nature. Not because of this, but only for the sake of sins he could claim this title. The sinful angels are not all from one choir, but angels fell from all of them, and many of them.

Now I want to report, as I saw it, after which honors and advantages Lucifer sought full of envy and pride. In the works of God everything is ordered according to measure, number and weight. Therefore, Divine Providence decided to reveal to the angels, immediately after their creation - that is, before they could turn to other goals - the final goal for which they had been created and endowed with such a sublime and excellent nature. God enlightened them in the following way: First, they received a very impressive knowledge of the essence of God, His unity in nature, His trinity in person. At the same time, they received the command to worship and adore the infinite God as their Creator and Lord. The good angels followed out of love and righteousness. They submitted themselves with the best will, received with faith what exceeded their power of comprehension, and obeyed joyfully. Lucifer, however, submitted only because the opposite seemed impossible to him, therefore not out of full love. He divided his will between himself and the infallible truth of the Lord. Therefore, he found the commandment difficult and troublesome, and he did not fulfill it with perfect love and not out of justice. Therefore, he got into a condition that brought about his disobedience. The nonchalance and restraint with which he performed these first acts did not yet deprive him of grace, but here his evil condition began. He felt a certain weakness in virtue and a sinking in spirit, and his radiant beauty diminished. In my opinion, the effect of this unkindness and lukewarmness is comparable to that which is produced in a soul by a voluntary venial sin, By this I do not mean to say that Lucifer was already sinning gravely or even venially at that time. He fulfilled God's commandments lukewarmly and imperfectly. This was his first step to the fall.

Furthermore, God revealed to the angels that he wanted to create humans, rational creatures of a lower order. These, too, were to love, fear and honor God as their author and their eternal good. He would exceedingly grace this nature. The second person of the most holy Trinity himself would become man and in hypostatic union unite the human nature with the divine one to one person. This future God-man shall be recognized, venerated and worshipped by the angels not only because of His divinity, but also because of His humanity, as their head. As subordinated to Him in dignity and grace, they were to be His servants. At the same time, God made the angels realize how proper, just and reasonable this submission was: for the acceptance of the foreseen merits of the God-Man had earned for them the grace they already possessed, as well as the glory they were yet to possess. Like all other creatures, they too had the task of glorifying the God-Man, because He was King of all beings. All rational creatures, capable of the knowledge and enjoyment of God, should become His people and acknowledge and worship Him as their head. Then the corresponding commandment was given to the angels.

The obedient, holy angels immediately submitted to this command with all their willpower, with humble and loving zeal. Lucifer, however, full of envy and puffed-up pride, resisted and urged the like-minded angels to do the same. They also disobeyed the divine command. **In return, Lucifer promised them that he would be their head and establish an independent principality against Christ**. Envy and arrogance and disorderly desire caused such delusion in these angels that he infected countless with the plague of sin.

Now that great battle arose in heaven, of which St. John reports. The obedient holy angels were inflamed with zeal to defend the honor of the Most High and the honor of the God-Man, whom they saw in one face. They asked for permission and authorization from the Lord to fight against the dragon. This was granted to them. - When all the angels were commanded to obey the incarnate Word, they received as a third commandment to acknowledge as mistress that woman in whose womb the only begotten of the Father was to take on human flesh. This woman would be their queen and the mistress of all creatures, surpassing in grace and glory all angels and men. The good angels distinguished themselves by accepting this command. They believed and praised in deepest humility the power and secrets of the Most High. Lucifer and his followers, however, as a result of this command and at the revelation of this secret, rose up with increasing arrogance. In rageful fury Lucifer desired for himself the distinction of becoming the head of all angels and of the whole human race. If this was possible only by hypostatic union, it should be done on him.

In view of the low nature of the mother of the incarnated word, U.L woman, Lucifer resisted under gruesome blasphemies. In irrepressible anger he revolted against the author of such great miracles of grace. He incited his comrades and cried: "**These orders are unreasonable! My Highness is offended by them! Therefore I will persecute and exterminate this nature, which you look upon me with such great love and still want to grace so abundantly. For this I will use all my power and cunning.** I will bring down this woman, the mother of the word, from the height to which you intend to raise her. I will bring your plans to nothing!"

This pompous, vain pride provoked the Lord's anger. To Lucifer's shame He said, **"This woman, whom you will not honor, will crush your head, overcome you and bring you to naught. If through your pride death will come into the world, through her humility will come the life and salvation of men. They will receive that reward and those crowns which you have lost along with your following."**

Lucifer, with foolish pride, resisted everything that he understood of the divine will and His resolutions. **He threatened the whole human race.** The good angels recognized the righteous anger of the Most High against Lucifer and his followers. They fought against them with the weapons of understanding, justice and truth.
Then the Most High performed another mysterious miracle. After revealing to the angels the hypostatic union of the second person with humanity through enlightenment, He showed them the Most Blessed Virgin in a visionary image. He made them see the pure human nature in a most perfect woman. In her His omnipotence would work much more wonderfully than in all other mere creatures, since He would deposit in this woman all the gifts and graces of His right hand in an incomparably high degree. The vision of this image of the Queen of Heaven and Mother of the Divine Word was granted to all the angels, good and bad. This vision filled the good ones with wonder. They sang songs of praise and immediately, armed with fervent zeal and the invincible

shield of that sign, began to defend the honor of the Incarnate God and His Most Holy Mother. The dragon and his followers, on the contrary, flared up in an irreconcilable hatred against Christ and - His Virgin Mother. Then took place what is contained in the 12th chapter of the Secret Revelation.

So much for an excerpt from: Life of the Virgin Mother Mary, by Mary of Agreda, Volume 1, pages 106-114, Miriam Verlag, Josef Künzli, D-7893 Jestetten, ISBN 3-87449-128-5.

We must not forget:

1. rebellion against God brings eternal chastisement.
2. Lucifer wants to persecute people.
3. the virgin Mother of God, will crush Lucifer's head.

Lucifer was, in his works, very successful and he is today more than ever. Catherine Emmerich said that if the demons were material, nothing would grow on earth because the sun could not shine on the earth. Whoever doubts this fact can watch on the Internet: "Anneliese Michel and the statements of the demons". Recorded on audio tapes. Here is an excerpt:

Lucifer about himself, about other demons and about hell.

1) "I am damned because I did not want to serve God and wanted to be ruler myself, although I was a creature."

2) "I was in heaven, and above the rank of him who is on the table. (= image of the Archangel Michael.) Exorcist:

"You could be with the Cherubin!" Answer: "Yes, I was there too."

3) "I am the supreme one from down there; the Michael has overthrown me. Now I can't do anything to him. All hell belongs to me."

4) "I want to conquer the earth for myself. First I still make rich booty. I fill my kingdom. I'll get who I can get, you can count on it.

5) "I am the father of lies."

6) "I never stop fighting. We like it much better in the world. I fight for every soul just like that one (= Jesus)."

7) " Do you know why I fight like this? Because I was overthrown because of the people par excellence."

8) "Do you know who is ruling the world today? Not the one who sacrificed himself in the world! It is me! The ... (= Nazarene) most of them have left. So stupid! This is a small flock that has remained faithful to him."

9) "I never keep what I promise."

10) "I'll mess you guys up yet; I'm the Diabolus."

11) "I have more to testify. If the ... (= Mother of God) would not force me like this! The woman has crushed my head."

12) "I'll tell the truth if the ... forces me."

13) "The Judas I have taken. He is always in my service. He is damned. For he could have saved himself. He did not follow that, the Nazarene."

14) "The Nazarene always forgives when .... . The (Virgin Mary) has told him often enough to mend his ways."

15) Question from the exorcist, "Would he do it again?" Answer, "No, never!"

16) **"Judas has many followers."**

17) "With us there is no rest for all eternity; rest is there, above (= in heaven)."

18) "Do you know how it burns down there?"

19) "With us there is no obedience; that is only up there."

20) "With us there is no going back, never for all eternity. From us, no one can go back. There is no love; with us there is only hatred. We never have peace; we fight each other. We want to go up there too."

21) **"The enemies of the church are ours."**

22) "Pride leads people to ruin."

23) "When the world has ended, we will continue.

Then things will get worse. If you had any idea what it is like down there. The seer children of Fatima saw it. If you had any idea how it is with us. You would kneel day and night before the ... (tabernacle). **I have to say it because the High Lady is forcing me."**

The creation of man - original sin.

The book of Moses (Genesis) reports about the creation of the earth. God created Adam and Eve after his image.

The image of God, should stand out from the animal world. Adam became the lord of the world, the elements should obey him, Eve was created as his helper. And the Lord God commanded the man, saying, "Thou mayest eat of every tree of the garden, but of the tree of the knowledge of good and evil thou shalt not eat: for in the day that thou eatest thereof thou must surely die."

And she took of the fruit, and did eat, and gave of it also unto her husband that was with her, and he did eat. Gn.3.5

As punishment, Adam and Eve were placed by God on the level of animals and they had to die, as threatened.

But to the woman he said, "Much distress you shall have through pregnancy; bearing children with pain, yet desiring your husband; and he shall be your master."

And to the man (Adam) he said, **"Because you have obeyed your wife and eaten of the tree of which I forbade you to eat, - cursed be the field for your sake! laboriously you shall feed on it all your life; it shall bear thorns and thistles for you, and you shall eat the herb of the field.** In the sweat of thy face shalt thou eat thy bread, until thou return unto the field from whence thou wast taken: for dust thou art, and unto dust must thou return." Gn.3 15-19

GOD refers to Adam as "man" and Eve as "woman" and helpmate. So it is written in the 1st book of Moses, about the fall of man. Is reported only about the commandments and the punishments; no word about the reasons for the commandment. God, unfortunately, did not speak on a recording. We must believe the narrators, and there are many.

What does the LORD say, in his book, DER GOTTMENSCH; to Adam and Eve, Volume I, page 100:

"You know all the laws and mysteries of creation. But do not deny me the right to be the creator of man. To reproduce the human race, my love that lives in you is enough. Without sensual desire and rather through the heartbeat of love, it will give life to new Adams of the human race. I give you everything. Only this secret of the creation of man, I reserve for myself."

Satan wanted to rob man of this virginity of mind and with his serpent tongues caressed Eve's limbs and eyes, awakening in her thoughts and sensations that she did not know before, because wickedness, had not yet poisoned her.

"She saw" and seeing, she wanted to try. The flesh had been awakened. Oh, if only she had called upon God! If she had rushed to say," Father, I am sick. The serpent has flattered me and I am confused".

The Father would have cleansed her and healed her with a breath; as he had poured life into her. Thus he could also again infuse purity into her, and make her forget the poison of the serpent; nay, instill in her an aversion to the serpent, similar to the instinctive revulsion felt by those who have been afflicted with a disease and healed, against the same evil.

But Eve does not go to the father. Eve returns to the serpent. The sensation pleases her. "When she saw that the fruit of the tree was good for food and appeared beautiful and pleasing to the eye, she took the same and ate of it."

And "she understood", now the wickedness was in her bowels to apply her bite. Eve saw with new eyes and heard with new ears, the habits and the voices of the beasts; she desired with immoderate lust. **She began sin alone. She completed it with her companion. Therefore, the greater guilt is on the woman.**

Because of her, the man has become a rebel against God and has known fornication and death. Because of her, he no longer knew how to control the three realms:

That of the spirit, because he allowed the spirit to rebel against God;

that of the moral conduct, because he allowed the passions to dominate him;

that of the flesh, because he degraded it to the instinctive laws of unreasoning animals."

Adam and Eve robbed the Father, the mystery of the creation of man. This was the original sin. The punishments were death, loss of dominion over the elements, painful birth and "by the sweat of thy face shalt thou earn thy bread".

The poison of the serpent continues to work in all people to this day. **Only God can cleanse and heal us, through a special grace.**

Some enjoy the poison as a drug and cultivate it in multiple perversions, others ask the almighty Father to make the poison in us harmless.

In spite of original sin, people have been allowed to keep something divine: **It is free will. Free will leads us, according to our thoughts and works, to heaven or hell.** Who does not bring the commanded respect and love to God all his life long, lives with Lucifer and has not directed his will to his creator.

God wanted to cause the descendants, by his love which lives in us. By a special grace, the Mother of God was born without hereditary guilt. **Without sensual desire, but with the heartbeat of God's love, Jesus, the Son of God, was born under the heart of Mary. As Lord over the elements, like Adam and Eve before him, he could enter the world without hurting his mother.**

In massless desire Adam and Eve begot their son Cain. In massless pain the birth takes place. Adam and Eve had lost the dominion over the elements (painless birth); Cain became the murderer of his brother.

Lucifer and his demons were and are very successful, today more than ever. Catherine Emmerich said that if the demons were material, there would be no growth on earth because the sun could not shine on the earth.

God's punishments in an overview.

1. The access to heaven was closed.

2. the righteous had to wait in limbo for their salvation.

3. dust you are, dust you shall become. We must die.

4. the woman shall give birth in pain.

5. man must earn his bread with toil.

6. mankind departed from God and became the plaything of demons.

- Isaiah 45.8 Dew ye heavens... and the Church knows the Rorate Mass before Christmas. It belongs to the realm of tradition, The Church sings: "Dew heavens to the righteous".

The Flood -- the wickedness of man Genesis 6. 1- 29

When men began to multiply over the earth and daughters were born to them, the sons of the gods saw how beautiful the daughters of men were, and they took wives from them as they pleased.

Then said the Lord: My spirit shall not abide forever in man, because he is also flesh, therefore his lifetime shall be one hundred and twenty years.

In those days there were giants on the earth, and even later, after the sons of the gods had become involved with the daughters of men and had given birth to these children. These are the heroes of the ancient times, the famous men.

The Lord saw that on earth the wickedness of the people increased and that all thinking and striving of his heart was always only evil.

Then it repented the Lord to have made man on earth, and it hurt his heart.

The Lord said: I will destroy the man whom I have created from the face of the earth, and with him also the cattle, the creeping things and the birds of the air, for it repented me to have made them.

Only Noah found favor in the eyes of the Lord.

Noah was a righteous, blameless man among his contemporaries; he went his way with God.

Noah begat three sons, Shem, Ham and Japheth.

The earth was corrupt in God's eyes; it was full of violence. God looked at the earth: It was corrupt, for all creatures of flesh on earth, lived corruptly. God said to Noah:

"Make yourself an ark of cypress wood! Equip it with chambers, and seal it inside and out with pitch!" Thus shalt thou build the ark:

"Three hundred cubits long, fifty cubits wide and thirty cubits high it shall be. Make a roof for the ark and raise it up exactly one cubit. Put the entrance of the ark on the side. Set up a lower floor, a second floor, and a third floor."

For I will bring the flood upon the earth to destroy every creature of flesh under heaven, everything that has spirit of life in it. Everything on earth shall perish.

But with you I make my covenant. Go into the ark, you, your sons, your wife and your sons' wives! Of all that lives, of all creatures of flesh, bring two each into your ark, that they may live with you; one male and one female.

Take with thee of every eatable thing, and lay up a store for thee. It shall be food for you and for them.

Noah did everything exactly as God had instructed him.

7.1-5 God said to Noah:

"Go thou into the ark with all thy family; for I have found thee alone righteous before me among this generation. Of all the clean animals take thee seven each, male and female, and of the unclean animals two each, male and female; also of the birds seven each, male and female, that offspring may live upon all the earth. For yet seven days, then will I cause to rain upon the earth forty days and forty nights, and will destroy from the face of the earth all that I have made." Noah did as God had commanded him.

The flood

7.17-24 Now the flood poured over the earth for forty days. The waters swelled and lifted up the ark so that it floated above the earth. And the waters became mighty, and increased greatly above the earth. But the ark sailed on the water. And mightier and mightier grew the waters above the earth. So that all the high mountains under the whole heaven were covered. Fifteen cubits high stood the water above them, so high were the mountains covered. Then all flesh perished that moves on the earth, birds, cattle, game, everything that teems on the earth, and all people. Everything that had breath of life in its nostrils, everything that lived on the land, died. Thus he destroyed every living thing that was on the earth, from man to cattle, to worms, and to the birds of the air. They were wiped out from the earth. Only Noah remained and what was with him in the ark. The water rose above the earth a hundred and fifty days.

The redemption of the righteous through Jesus Christ

The souls of the righteous deceased, gathered in the crypts of limbo and waited devotedly for the promised redemption, through the Messiah. If science has not made a mistake, 4,000 years have passed since the Fall, until the birth of Jesus. For Adam and Eve, and their righteous descendants, a long time. But also the grandparents of Jesus, Anna and Joachim, had to endure in the uncomfortable place. The question of salvation has always occupied theologians. Martin Luther was of the opinion that through the death of the Lord on the cross, all people were redeemed. The Lord Himself answered this question in His book, DER GOTTMENSCH. Volume XII page 175.

Jesus says: "Give me your full attention, for I have to tell you extraordinarily important things. You will not yet understand them all, or understand them not quite correctly. But he who comes after me will enlighten you. So listen to me.

No one is more convinced than you that man sins very easily without God's help, because his constitution, weakened by sin, is very vulnerable. **I would therefore be an unwise redeemer if, having given you so much to redeem you, I did not also give you the means to preserve the fruits of my sacrifice.** You know that the ease of sinning comes from original sin, which deprives people of grace and therefore of their strength of soul: **union with God.**

You have said, "But you have restored grace (salvation) to men" No. **It has been restored (only) to the righteous until my death. In order to restore it to future people, a means is needed. A means that will not only be a ritual, but that will make all who receive it truly children of God. Just as Adam and Eve were, whose souls, animated by grace, possessed sublime graces. Which God had given to his beloved creatures**.

You know what man possessed and what he lost. **Now, through my sacrifice, the gates of grace are opened again, and the stream of grace can pour over all who ask for it out of love for me.** Therefore, people will have the quality of being children of God through the merits of the firstborn among men, the one who speaks to you, your Savior and eternal High Priest, your teacher and brother in the common Father. **In Jesus Christ and through Jesus Christ, the present and the future people, will be able to possess heaven and rejoice in God, the ultimate goal of man**. Until now, even the most righteous of the righteous could not reach this goal, although they too were circumcised as children of the chosen people. In spite of their God-approved virtues, and although their places in heaven were ready, yet it was closed and God's possession denied them, because on their souls, the blessed flowerbeds of all virtues, there also stood the accursed tree of original sin, and no work, however holy, could destroy it; and because one cannot enter heaven with the roots and foliage of a noxious plant.

On the day of preparation the groaning of the patriarchs and prophets, and of all the righteous of Israel, ceased, in the joy of accomplished redemption, and the souls, whiter than the mountain snow by their virtues, were now pure from the only stain that separated them from heaven. But life in the world goes on. Generations come and go. New peoples will always come to Christ. And can Christ die for each new generation to redeem them, or for each people to come to Him? No. Christ died once and will not die again for eternity. Shall these generations, then, these peoples, become knowledgeable through my word, but not be allowed to possess heaven and behold God because they are stained by original sin? No. That would not be just, neither to them, whose love for me would be in vain, nor to me, who would then have died for far too little.

But do you remember what I did that night, even though you were already outwardly pure? I tied a linen cloth around myself and washed your feet, and to one of you, who was excited by this humiliating gesture, I said: "If I don't wash you, you will have no part with me". You did not understand what I was saying, what share I meant, what symbol this was. Well, this is how I want to tell you.

I have not only taught you that humility and purity are necessary to enter the Kingdom of Heaven and have a share in my Kingdom. I have not only pointed out to you with kindness that God requires from a righteous person, who is thus pure in spirit and mind, only a final washing of that part which, by nature, is most easily defiled even among the righteous, even if only by the dust which the necessary coexistence with men leaves on the pure members, the flesh, but I have pointed out to you something else. I have washed your feet, the lowest part of the body, which goes through mud and dust, perhaps also through dirt, and have meant by this the flesh, the material part of man, which always - except in those who are free from the stain of original sin by the working of God or the divine nature - has imperfections. They are sometimes so small that only God sees them; nevertheless, you must watch over them so that they do not grow and become a habit, and you must fight them to eradicate them.

So I have washed your feet. Why? Before I broke the bread and changed it with the wine into my flesh and blood. Because **I am the Lamb of God and cannot come where Satan has left his mark**. Therefore, I have cleansed you beforehand. Then I gave myself. You also, through baptism, will wash those who come to me, so that they will not receive my body unworthily and this will not become a terrible death sentence for them.

You are dismayed. You look at each other. Your eyes ask: "And Judas?" I tell you, **"Judas has eaten his death"**. This supreme act of love has not touched his heart. His Master's last attempt bounced off the stone of his heart, and that stone bore, instead of the dew, the terrible seal of Satan carved on it, the mark of the beast.

So I washed you before I admitted you to the Eucharistic meal and received the confession of your sins, before I poured the Holy Spirit into you and thus confirmed you as true Christians in grace and as my priests. And so it shall be with all others whom you will prepare for the Christian life.

Baptize with water in the name of the One and the Triune and in my name, so that through my inexhaustible merits, the original debt in the hearts may be erased, the sins may be forgiven, the graces and the holy virtues may be infused, and the Holy Spirit may descend and take up residence in the consecrated temples that will be the bodies of the people living in the grace of the Lord. Was the water necessary to blot out sin? The water does not touch the soul, no. But a non-material sign is not seen by man, who is so related to matter in all his works. Even without a visible sign, I could have poured life.
But who would have believed it then? How many people can believe unshakably even if they do not see?
Therefore, take from the old Mosaic law the pure water with which one washes the unclean, in order to be able to admit them again to the meetings after they have defiled themselves on a corpse. In truth, every person who is born is defiled because he comes into contact with a soul that has died to grace. He must therefore be cleansed from the impure touch with the purifying water in order to become worthy to enter the eternal temple.

Hold the water in honor...Having atoned and redeemed through thirty-three years of arduous life culminating in the Passion, having given all my blood for the sins of men, from the bled and spent body of the martyr flowed the healing waters that wash away original sin. With the accomplished sacrifice, I have redeemed you from this stain. If I had risen from the cross at the threshold of life, by one of my divine miracles, truly I tell you, by the shed blood I would have cleansed you from your sins, but not from the original sin. For them, the sacrifice made to the end was necessary. Verily, the healing waters of which Ezekiel speaks have flowed from this side wound of mine. **Immerse your soul in these waters so that they may come out of them unblemished to receive the Holy Spirit.** He will breathe and dwell again in the souls of redeemed people in remembrance of the breath by which the Creator gave Adam a soul and thus made him in His image and likeness.

Baptize with my baptism, but in the name of the Triune God; for in truth I tell you, had the Father not willed and the Spirit not cooperated, the Word would not have become flesh and there would have been no redemption. Therefore, it is just and proper that in baptism a man should receive life through those who have united their wills to give it to him: the Father, the Son, and the Holy Spirit, and that the baptized should receive from me the name of Christ, to distinguish this rite from the others, past and future, which are rites but do not imprint an indelible mark on the immortal part.

And take the bread and the wine, as I have done, and bless, divide, and distribute them in my name; and let the Christians be satisfied with me. Offer the bread and wine to the Father in heaven, and then consume them in remembrance of the sacrifice which I offered for your salvation and accomplished on the cross. **You, my priests, should do this in memory of me, so that the inexhaustible treasures of my sacrifice may imploringly ascend to God and descend beneficially upon those who ask for it with firm faith.**

With firm faith, I say, No science is necessary to partake of the Eucharistic food and sacrifice. **Only faith! Only faith that the bread and the wine that one who is empowered by me or by those who come after me -** you, Peter, new pontiff of the new Church, you, James the Alphaeus, you, John, you, Andrew, you. Simon, you, Bartholomew, you, Thomas, you, Judas Thaddeus, you Matthew, you, Jacob of Zebedee-**blessing in my name are my true body and blood; that whoever receives them for food and drink receives me with flesh and blood, soul and divinity; that whoever offers me really offers Jesus Christ, as he offered himself for the sins of the world.**

A child or an ignorant person can receive me as well as a scholar or an adult. And a child and an ignorant person will have the same benefit from the offered sacrifice as each of you has. **It is enough that they believe and have the grace of the Lord.**

But you will still receive a new baptism: The baptism of the Holy Spirit. I have promised it to you, and it will be given to you. The Holy Spirit Himself will descend upon you. I will tell you when. And you will be filled with him, in the fullness of the priestly gift. You will therefore be able to pass on the Holy Spirit, by whom you will be filled, as I did with you, in order to strengthen Christians in grace and to transmit to them the gifts of the Paraclete (Holy Spirit in Confirmation).

The royal sacrament, (Confirmation) which is only slightly inferior to that of the ordination of priests, is to be administered solemnly, like the Mosaic ordinations, by the laying on of hands and anointing with fragrant oil, as was formerly used for the ordination of priests. No, don't look at me so frightened! I am not saying sacrilegious words. I do not teach you sacrilegious works! **The dignity of the Christian is, I repeat, only a little less than that of the priests.**

Where do the priests live? In the temple. And a Christian will be a living temple. What do the priests do? They serve God through prayer, sacrifice and care for the faithful. At least that's how it should have been...And the Christian serves God through prayer, sacrifice and brotherly love. And you will listen to the confession of sins, as I have listened to and forgiven yours and the sins of many, when I have seen true repentance.

You are troubled? Why? Are you afraid of not being able to distinguish? I have already spoken several times about sin and about judging sin. But remember that in judging, you must pay attention to the seven conditions that make something be sin or not, and sin of different severity. To summarize: When and how often was sin committed; who sinned; with whom; what was the object of the sin; what was the cause; why was sin committed.

Do not be afraid. The Holy Spirit will assist you. **What I ask of you with all my heart is that you live a holy life.** This will increase the supernatural light in you, so that you can read people's hearts without being mistaken, and speak with love and authority to sinners who are afraid to expose their guilt. Or refuse to confess them and reveal the state of their soul; that you can help the timid and humble the unrepentant. Remember that the earth loses the one who forgives, and you shall be what I have been: just, patient and merciful, but not weak. **I have told you that whatever you bind on earth will be bound in heaven, and whatever you loose on earth will be loosed in heaven.** Therefore, you shall judge every man with proper consideration, without being influenced by affection or aversion, by gifts or threats, impartially in all and toward all, as God is, taking into account also the weaknesses of man and the reenactments of his enemies.

So much for the teaching of the LORD to His apostles and disciples.

The Lord said: "**In order to restore it (the grace of salvation) to future men, a means is needed. A means that will not be only a ritual, but that will make all who receive it truly children of God**". The Lord speaks of the Holy Sacrifice of the Mass.

He said: offer bread and wine to the Father in heaven and then consume them in memory of the sacrifice.

The Church of Jesus Christ and the Revolt

The Lord established His Church after His resurrection. Peter was called to be the visible head: **You are Peter, and upon this rock I will build My Church, and the gates of hell shall not prevail against it. I will give you the keys of the kingdom of heaven; whatever you bind on earth will be bound in heaven, and whatever you loose on earth will be loosed in heaven.** (Mt.16.18+19) The apostles were ordained bishops and the disciples priests. Their commission is: "**Go ye therefore, and teach all nations, baptizing them in the name of the Father, and of the Son, and of the Holy Ghost, teaching them to observe all things whatsoever I have commanded you. And behold, I am with you always, even to the end of the age**". Mt. 28: 19-20

Lucifer, the enemy of God and his creatures sounded: "**I will conquer the earth for myself. First I make still rich booty. I fill my kingdom. I fetch whom I can fetch, there you may rely on it.**" (Anneliese Michel)

Why does God give Lucifer this power? Does he need him to test us? Maybe! **We can resist Lucifer and his demons only if we live in the grace of God.**

"Blessed is the man that endureth temptation: for after he is tried, he shall receive the crown of life, which God hath promised to them that love him." (James 1.12)

Love for God, is essential in the successful fight against demons. To fight against the demons, He has given us the

Sacrifice of the Mass. For the sacrifice of the Mass, the Lord has appointed the priests.

With the bull "Quo primum" of 17.7.1570, the Missale Romanum was instituted by Pope Pius V, uniformly and irrevocably, for the Church. The bull ends with the warning:

"But if anyone should presume to touch this, let him know that he will incur the wrath of Almighty God and of His Holy Apostles Peter and Paul.

The Council of Trent teaches:

"Whoever says that in the Mass no true and proper sacrifice is offered to God, or that the act of sacrifice is nothing else than Christ being given to us for food, let him be charged with anathema (exclusion from the Church)."

The Lord taught His apostles and disciples:

"Now, through my sacrifice, the gates of grace are opened again, and the river of grace can be poured out on all who ask for it out of love for me".

In order to keep the doctrine, the rites and the tradition forever pure and unadulterated, in the year 678, a working document was drawn up for the Popes, the Coronation Oath of the Popes. The Coronation Oath has the following wording:

"I vow not to diminish, alter, or permit any innovation in the tradition, in what I have found preserved by my godly predecessors; rather, with fervent devotion as their truly faithful disciple and successor, to reverently preserve with all my strength and effort what has been handed down to me;. To purify everything that may appear contrary to the canonical order; to guard the sacred canons and ordinances of our popes as if they were divine mandates from heaven, since I am aware that I must give the strictest account of everything I confess to You, Whose place I take by divine grace, Whose substitution I hold with Your support, in the divine judgment.

If I should undertake to act in anything according to any other sense or allow it to be undertaken, You will not be merciful to me on that dreadful day of divine judgment.

Therefore, We also subject to the exclusion of strict ban: whoever should dare - be it We ourselves, be it another - to undertake anything new in contradiction to this so constituted evangelical tradition and the purity of the orthodox faith and the Christian religion, or should seek by his adverse efforts to change anything or to embezzle from the purity of the faith, or to consent to those who undertake such blasphemous venture."

The Coronation Oath of the Popes was instituted in 678 and was first administered in writing for about 600 years, and then orally until Paul VI, in Council. It is a promise made by the Vicar to the invisible head of the Church, Jesus Christ. This document was to ensure that the divine teachings and rites would be preserved, unchanged, in His Church.

Lucifer has always been active. His plan is to eradicate the priesthood and the sacrifice of the Mass. He was successful with Islam. He was able to wipe out the Christian strongholds in North Africa, in Spain and in Palestine, with the sword. In Russia and Germany, he succeeded in splitting the church. Popes, too, had lost sight of the Lord's mission.

Now it was a matter of: Ecrasez l`infâme, that was the call of Voltaires against the church. Crush the vile. Meant are the priesthood and the sacrifice of the mass. Lucifer successfully organizes a continuous infiltration of the Catholic Church.

On 24.6.1917 (Fatima year and Russian revolution) the Freemasons demanded on St. Peter's Square: **"Satan must rule in the Vatican, the Pope must be his slave".**

On October 28, 1958, the goal was achieved. Cardinal Angelo Guiseppe Roncalli, was elected the 261st Pope. He called himself John XXIII.

Gioele Magaldi, writes in his book, "La scoperta delle Ur-Lodges," that Roncalli was initiated into two lodges, in Paris. "He (Magaldi) hailed, for example, Vatican Council II as the fulfillment of (almost) all Masonic wishes. No wonder, he himself thought, since it was prepared and convened by the highest degree Mason, Angelo Roncalli alias Pope John XXIII, initiated in two different primitive lodges.

The Second Vatican Council, was opened on October 11, 1962 and closed on December 8, 1965. It was convened by Pope John XXIII with the mandate of pastoral and ecumenical "instauratio". Instauration means renewal, mending, restoration.

Renewal was not necessary, because the Lord did not give a new mission to His Church. The mission of the LORD had never changed.

With the vote on religious liberty, on 7.12.65, 2,400 bishops. condemned the teachings of four popes. The current canon law about heresy, was put aside. The coronation oath of the popes was also put aside, it disappeared very quickly from all textbooks. Most of the "Fathers of the Church" supported this betrayal, few of them were outraged to no effect. None spoke of heresy or excommunication. This resistance of the bishops, reminds of the test of the angels. .

Now, it was possible to set the decisive course. With the change of the episcopal consecration, it was possible to stop the priestly growth. With the change of the sacrifice of the Mass, the access to heaven could be closed again. What Lucifer succeeded in doing with Adam and Eve, he should succeed again here.

The Lord said: Now, through my sacrifice, the gates of grace are opened again, and the stream of grace can flow over all who ask for it out of love for me.

Lucifer had to change that. His episcopal assistants should invent a new rite, although a new rite, according to the bull Quo primun is not allowed. They invented the "memorial celebration"

In the memorial celebration there is no sacrifice for the Father. Nor may it be a sacrifice if the desired end is to be achieved; and so after the consecration the deacon declares, "Thy death O Lord we proclaim, thy resurrection we praise, until thou come in glory."

The Council of Trent teaches:

"Whoever says that in the Mass no true and proper sacrifice is offered to God, or that the sacrificial act is nothing else than that Christ is given to us as food, shall be charged with anathema (exclusion from the Church)".

In the Coronation Oath, the Pope vowed:

"Therefore, We also subject to exclusion the severe ban: whoever should dare - be it We ourselves, be it another - to undertake anything new in contradiction to this evangelical tradition thus constituted and to the purity of the orthodox faith and the Christian religion, or should strive by his adverse efforts to change anything, or to embezzle from the purity of the faith, or to agree with those who undertake such blasphemous daring."

Lucifer boasted, "Do you know who rules in the world today? Not the one who sacrificed himself in the world! It is I! The ... (= Nazarene) has been abandoned by most. So stupid! This is a small flock that has remained faithful to Him."

Yes, we know and see it. Lucifer rules the Church, politics, television and the Internet, the press, schools, associations, families and education, in short, the whole world.

We also know the Canon Law:

Canon 1364 § 1: "The apostate, the heretic, or the schismatic incur excommunication as a penalty of crime."

There is no need for a court, no accusation, the guilty person incurs the penalty of excommunication himself.

Canon 1374 : "Whoever joins an association that engages in machinations against the Church shall be subject to just punishment; but whoever promotes or directs such an association shall be punished by interdict."

Can. 1331 § 1. The excommunicated person is forbidden:

1. any service in the celebration of the Eucharistic Sacrifice or in any other worship celebrations;

2. to administer sacraments or sacramentals and to receive sacraments.

The betrayal of the Church is egregious and indisputable. Religious liberty, memorial service, coronation oath, freemasonry, etc., etc., everywhere Satan has left his mark and leads the church on a short leash.

The Lord says: **The Lamb of God cannot come where Satan has left his traces**.

Every believer can now easily find out where the church and the priests stand, and where he himself stands.

With our spirit we can not only sin, we can also do valuable good works. Prayer.

We are not without guidance. The Lord says, "What I ask of you with all my heart is that you live holy lives!"

"Immerse your soul in this water, ((water from the sidewall) that they may come out of it spotless, to receive the Holy Spirit."

"It is enough that they believe and have the grace of the Lord".

"He who sacrifices me, truly sacrifices Jesus Christ",

"The dignity of the Christian is, I repeat, only slightly inferior to that of the priests".

Sacrifice, then, the Precious Blood several times a day for the sins of the world and pray:

Father in heaven, I offer up to you the Body and Blood, the Soul and Divinity, of our Lord Jesus Christ, in reparation for my sins and the sins of the whole world.

Accept Father this sacrifice also, with every beat of my heart, as a perpetual atonement, for the conversion of sinners, the salvation of the dying, the redemption of the poor souls in purgatory, and banish Satan and all evil spirits to hell.

Let us worship the offending and reviled majesty of God. Let us atone for the many sins.

Infinitely holy God... infinitely merciful Father! I adore You. I want to atone for the dishonor inflicted on You by sinners everywhere on earth and at every moment of the day and night. Above all, let me make reparation for the insults and sins that are being committed in this hour. I offer Thee the adoration and expiation of those souls who love Thee. I offer Thee, above all, the perpetual sacrifice of Thy divine Son. Who offers Himself on our altars throughout the world and at every moment. Infinitely good and mild Father! Take up the most pure Blood of Jesus Christ in reparation for man's offenses: blot out their sins and show them mercy.

The daily Rosary is an indispensable, powerful aid.

Fatima

Our Lady said to the visionary children in Fatima on July 13, 1917: "You have seen the hell toward which poor sinners are heading. To save them, the Lord wants to introduce devotion to my Immaculate Heart in the world. If one does what I tell you, many soule

s will be saved and peace will come. The war is coming to an end, but if you do not stop offending the Lord, it will not be long before another one, even worse, begins; it will happen during the pontificate of Pius XI. If then one night you will see an unknown light, know that it is the sign from GOD that the punishment of the world for its many crimes is near: war, famine and persecution of the Church and the Holy Father.

To prevent this, I will (come and) ask to consecrate Russia to my Immaculate Heart and to introduce the Communion of Atonement on the first Saturday of the month.

If my request is fulfilled, Russia will be converted and there will be peace. If not, it (Russia) will spread its errors in the world, cause war and persecutions of the Church; the good will be martyred, the Holy Father will suffer much; several nations will be destroyed....In the end, my Immaculate Heart will triumph, the Holy Father will consecrate to me Russia, which will convert, and the world will be given some time of peace."

Excerpt from: "Mary Speaks to the World" by Prof. Dr. L. Gonzaga da Fonseca, 1963, page 45.

On 6/13/1929, 10 years before World War 2, Sister Lucia writes in Tuy: "Our Lady said: page 196:

"The time has come when, according to the desire of the Lord, the Holy Father, in union with all the bishops of the world, should consecrate Russia to my Immaculate Heart; for this he promises to save it by this means."

Inconceivably, the request of the Lord, delivered by the Mother of God, Queen of the Church, was not fulfilled by Pope Pius XI from 1922 to 1939.

A conversion of Russia, would have destroyed a work of Satan, united the Orthodox with the Christians and "the world will be given some time of peace".

The opposite occurred, there was the 2nd World War, the punishment threatened by Our Lady in Fatima. Satan rules the whole world. The world is in a satanic paralysis.

What can be said about the consecration of Russia, by Francis, of 3/25/2022?

What did Our Lady say to the children in Fatima?

In the end, my Immaculate Heart will triumph and the Holy Father will consecrate Russia to me.

She spoke of two events that will happen at the "end".

1st event: In the end, my Immaculate Heart will triumph.

2nd event: The Holy Father will consecrate Russia to me.

According to this statement of Our Lady, first comes the triumph of the Immaculate Heart and only after that comes the consecration of Russia.

What could Our Lady, in the last 100 years, triumph over? Rome has lost the faith, the Catholic Church of the Lord has degenerated into a sect that is under the divine curse.

All this is no reason to triumph. Our Lady wished the consecration of Russia by the Holy Father in union with all the bishops of the world.

On 25.3.2022, the Council sect, which is under the divine curse, gathered in Rome. A sect has neither a Holy Father nor bishops.

The Catholics are without priestly leadership. Can the few faithful, successfully fight against Satan or must the Lord Himself intervene to restore the old, Tridentine order?

If we would put aside our indifference and in the grace of God, join our forces, we could count on God's help and win the battle. Without the grace of God, we will be paralyzed by Lucifer. It is in our hands. The daily offering of the Precious Blood and the Rosary can help.